WINGED

poems by

Sarah Grieve

Finishing Line Press
Georgetown, Kentucky

WINGED

ACKNOWLEDGMENTS

I would like to thank these magazines and presses for giving homes to
versions of the poems in this collection: *Apalachee Review* ("Ode to Kevin
Costner in *Bull Durham*" & "Plate Appearances"), *Bayou* ("Under the
Condor"), *Cimarron Review* ("Sarah Winchester's Sestina in Thirteens"),
A Face to Meet the Faces: An Anthology of Contemporary Persona Poems
("Calamity Jane Informs Wild Bill of His Faults While Visiting his Grave"),
The Missouri Review Online ("Ode in a Bikini"), *New Madrid* ("The Age
of Generosity"), *New Ohio Review* ("What I'll Settle For"), *RATTLE* ("The
Rules, published as "To Old Men"), *The Sow's Ear Poetry Review* ("Daphne
in the Rain, published as "Finding the Borghese Museum in Rome"), and
Waxwing ("Rerouted Due to Weather" and "The Hibiscus"). A number of
these poems appeared as part of the chapbook *Honey My Tongue* published
by Palooka Press (2014).

Publisher: Leah Maines

Editor: Christen Kincaid

Cover Art: Grace Wenzel Berscht

Author Photo: Calvin James Emerson

Cover Design: Elizabeth Maines McCleavy

Printed in the USA on acid-free paper.
Order online: www.finishinglinepress.com
also available on amazon.com

Author inquiries and mail orders:
Finishing Line Press
P. O. Box 1626
Georgetown, Kentucky 40324
U. S. A.

Table of Contents

for Adam,
the one for whom these poems always longed.

One

Rerouted Due to Weather

"For a language to survive, it's got to be spoken by men and women in bed."
—*Welsh poet Gwyneth Lewis*

The sheets are full of punctuation—dashes
    and colons, once randy, have rolled over
and we didn't notice, just as we didn't notice
    when the police chopper filled our motel window
with its search light, the pilot mistaking us
    for meth dealers who stay at seedy dive hotels
to cook up a deal or peddle their wares
    because if we were criminals or ne'er-do-wells,
we wouldn't define *wonky* and *kumquat*
    and *cattywombus* in the mornings when floor boards
cackle and snap, when stray dogs scratch at doors
    trying to find the welcome mat they remember;
we wouldn't leave the motel and sit at LAX
    watching the screens announce take-offs and delays,
guessing at the Buenos Aires bound briefs
    in leopard-printed suitcases, and wanting all things
translated into another language, one that turns
    waiting list into *lista de espera, espera* the feather
of the phrase, tumbling in its descent, lilting
    soft on the tongue the way you used to tell me, *breathe,*
as if saying it would send air through my lungs,
    expand my capillaries, open my pores so words
like *chaparral* and *chinchilla* could fill me, shine
    light upon our nakedness—once again, the sighs
and commas simmering between us saying,
    Vieni con me. Suivez-moi. Come on. Let's go.

The Age of Generosity

A homeless man stopped me on the street, not to ask
for change or beg a meal but to remark, *You're tall,*

I think that's sexy. Want a potato chip? I stumbled
into the gutter, nodding at him sideways as I left,

and later, when I mentioned it to my friend, we laughed
in a pitch we hadn't reached since the first time a boy

looked up our skirts and we kind of liked it. She told me
about the guy in Rome yelling, *How's the air up there?*

You breathe like a goddess, which sounded better, dirtier
in Italian, and then we talked about meeting Jack LaLanne,

how he leaned over our table, purring, *You ladies, your bodies
look quite fit,* patting our knees as his wife looked on. Now,

years later, I remember how we smiled at Jack, at all men,
collecting compliments like lemon drops from an open

candy tin, sure to find it refilled whenever we wanted more,
and I want to tell my former-self to suck hard on the whistles,

wedge them between teeth and cheek until only a sliver
remains, the jagged piece finally slipping down my throat.

Sometimes I try to picture an old man thrusting a half-full bag
of chips at the 20 year-old me, and if I could do it all again,

I like to think I'd stop, dig my hand in saying, *These chips
look damn good*—my lips soon to be heavy with salt and grease.

Ode in a Bikini

No, Sun, I won't try on that after-summer swimsuit,
      and it has nothing to do with the mismatched neon lycra
and sticky panty liners I'll have to wade through
      or that the suit is cheap and leftover. I could get past the color:
butterstick—worse, butter in the pan too long, butter and garlic

burnt and browned—when even Doris Day yellow makes me
      look like an undead queen recently risen from the underworld,
but I'm not wearing a one-piece, not now or soon, because my boobs
      are too damned wild to be masked beneath the suction
of respectable swimwear—we, my boobs and I, want to be dusted
      with dry sand, nicked with your rays, and I'm not looking

for function (there's plenty of time for that), I want to dive
      under water, somersault and back flip with the chance
of a nipple escaping, want to feel men's nipple-gazing,
      because in the dervish-ness of it all, I'll see their jazz,
see the way I feel when the lace of my bra shows through,

but then I'll stuff myself back in, straighten sunglasses
      and congress with the other bikini-clad women and their breasts
and navels, their bare backs and scantily clad asses because we're not
      the ones sitting beneath umbrellas, sipping on orange juice
instead of Sangria and Singapore Slings, not yet. Don't you see?
      Every woman hates herself from behind, or at least that's what

Cindy Crawford said and she should know, and even if I do,
      (I do), even if you, too, hate my backside and want nothing more
than to smooth out my dimples and hips like deburring the edges
      of machined metal, I'll still bare skin, uncover my middle,
untie the strings, trip up surfers and lifeguards as they survey

the horizon. O Sun, freckle and burn me, let me feel the full force
      of your licks because one day you'll hurt me, scavenge
and scar me, leave me to cover up with long sleeves and pant legs.
      It won't be your fault I've lured and chased you, asked you
to sweat me each high-noon. Just let me feel the weight of your touch,
      the heft of you over me until the hulk of dusk surrounds me.

Family Snapshot: Betty & Bobsi

—Los Angeles, June 7, 1931

Two girls sit on a cart in light smocks, noon sun
        on backs and bangs. To the right, a pony should be pulling
the rig on waist-high wheels—the older girl's feet scuff
        floorboard, but her sister's don't touch. They smirk,
though no teeth show because it's '31 and economy

has taught them a certain clutching of things.
        They've made it down the coast, just over the hill
from the chauffeurs of Grauman's and the Brown Derby,
        places they won't see for years and wars—but that day
it's an ostrich in front of the wagon, the bird's plumage

and spindle legs just separate from the shrubs. Its head,
        a sock puppet limb, points forward, but in real time
it would have weaved while the claw-foot pawed dirt,
        threatening. The beast should be amongst those animals
not yet of this world—griffins and centaurs—made

out of backward can-can knees and petticoat feathers,
        but it's the ostrich's bites and kicks these girls recognize:
the restrained strikes and rein-held trot long gone on days
        when Dad got paid. Beyond the photographer's flash,
the smaller girl's whisper practiced in those distant dawns:

"Quiet now." Her plea never whittling the man's nerve,
        but I have to think the bird, there, must have stalled,
folded its feathers, and mired us all to that spot—
        the photo a collection of slammed-door-late-night
shreddings swept into a rusted dust pan.

The Rules

"No, you cannot borrow my t-shirt. How about instead of standing there looking shocked, you do your fucking laundry?"
                                        —The Twitter page @shitmydadsays

While my father doesn't use that type of language, he makes
        similar demands about dress: guys who wear bowties
can't be trusted because bowties are as insincere
        as a bouquet of baby's breath or bringing store-bought
fruitcake to Christmas. For him, a baseball cap
        can only be worn backwards after catching seven innings;
just two men in the history of basketball, Wilt the Stilt
        and Slick Watts, had heads round enough to sport
sweatbands; and suspenders belong on men over 40
        or no one at all. I often think these things when I meet men,
making mental lists of their faults: the gaps in their teeth,
        the wheeze that escapes when they exhale, and I wonder
if old men have it right, if the catalogues created
        in the easy-chairs of their retirement are less self-indulgent
and more sage because nine times out of ten I don't answer
        the call for a second date. It isn't because the guy's hair
is too long or his car needs to be washed or he holds his fork
        like it's a twig used to poke at chicken carcasses. Despite
his ability to fix the faucet and calculate the tip in his head,
        I don't call because in his joints-aching, reading-glasses-wearing,
stick-it-to you days, I can't envision that guy turning up
        the volume on the television just to yell over it, "Athletes
should never be allowed to wear baggy uniforms
        because the league should have some goddamn standards,"
and there *should* be standards and all announcers
        should call the game like Vin Scully or Johnny Most
but most today can't, which leads Justin's dad to tweet,
        "Do these announcers ever shut the fuck up? Don't ever say
stuff just because you think you should," and it is that quiet
        between questions, the ability to let conversation collect
like raindrops in an open basin that most young guys
        fail to understand and that's what I want and what most
old men know: how to speak with a pop like wood on a ball
        and how it takes them less than 140 characters to write

what they mean and how tying a tie or buttoning a shirt
        has a purpose and should be done correctly, and if it is,
if it all matches up, then you might have something to say.

To Simonetta

The first time you sat for Botticelli, did you know you'd feed men
in deep pulls of oil, sweeps of paint? Did you want to strip for him then,
to reveal the contour of limb, length of neck plunging to breast

like cypress to earth, to give them la bella Simonetta, "the unparalleled one"
they wanted you to be? It's said you flung nipples and lips their way
in return for verse, song, or statue—I wonder if you expected him

to wrench corset and bodice from you in search of his muse,
to use your sweat to season his canvas the way a cook pours olive oil
in a new skillet. But, he didn't—didn't touch the gauze of your robe,

left your hair unfingered, tousled only by the force of his gaze.
He gave them only your best parts, the choicest cuts, the pieces
found roiled in women of royalty and myth that he whip-stitched

to the membranes and casings cradling your organs. Was it then
you unfurled, believing that canticles waft from the Duomo
to save us, cling in the space between ear and skull waiting

to urge or warn? When painted quiet, could you hear
the gristle of his tools crafting your ribcage from the roll of *le colline,*
your toes from *piccioni* atop spires? I, too, want to be wrapped

in the wind god's mist, linger until the sun slinks away
and the clam turns to sand speckled with fish bones, but men
only paint the asp slipping its tongue in my ear, care too much

for the palette of my thigh. Watch, I'll collect drops of dye and pigment
on my tongue, swallow the colors until my lungs are so full of art,
I choke—sputtering and keening to create myself in the flesh.

Ode to Bad First Dates

You stood me up, called months later,
            quizzed me on the differences between
labiodentals and voiced fricatives, took me
                        to see a play at a theater that's been closed
for a year, ate all my chocolate mousse
            while I was in the bathroom, and still,

I find you at hole-in-the-wall pubs,
            art galleries, and church league ball games.
Just when I think I've outwitted your plans
                        to stalk me, finally struck a deal
with the deities of dating, I end up
            on your front porch again where you dodge

my attempt to kiss you, and shut the door
            before I can blurt out the obligatory,
Nice to meet you. I've heard it said,
                        "You have the love life you want,"
and if that's true, you and I must be engaged
            in some strange sado tryst because there is no

spooning or crooning, no cooing here,
            just the business end of ice picks
and curling irons. I know I should be grateful
                        for your company, forgive the bunch
of marigolds you picked from my neighbor's
            walkway—these are small potatoes

in the long line of mammoth spuds
            filling many girls' shopping baskets. I'm not
waiting for my fingertips to tingle
                        or the rib cage tightening magic
that will spring according to the voiceovers
            of online dating ads, but if I do stop

expecting your call, will I end up in the empty
            drag of winter's half light? No one cares
for you like I do, baby, tells your story
                    with the same marionette mad-jerk gestures,
exaggerates your very best bits, but surely,
            one day, I'll look up from a half-written

grocery list at the sound of a fiancé's key
            in my door and think of our nights of clasp
and swelter, the waking with booze-heavy
                    breath, my eyes a mess of black-liner smudge—
these now only revelries held in the moment before
            I dip my head to sink, splash my face, apologize for going.

Self-Portrait Near Thirty

Jewelry certainly, though not a ring or brooch—
      a locket maybe, gold and patinaed: at ten,
you slid it, your first belonging of real worth,
      into a matchbox, stuck it in your pink music box
and wrapped the whole thing in the morning's
      LA Times—the day the headline read "DIANA DEAD,"
the day your mother braced against the plush
      of the sofa headed directly for the wall
of the Pont de l'Alma tunnel. It was then you understood
      break neck speed, sent your girlhood
treasure to swim in the peanuts of a mailing box
      that it might avoid that abrasion, later excision.
You'd read about the Veronese volunteers who answer
      every piece of mail addressed to Juliet, and so you pictured
a secretary in the dead letter office of another country—
      one of motion, perpetual or spondic: Jakarta, Melbourne,
Rio, Juneau, Stockholm, even La Paz—someone who fit
      the addressee you scrawled: "To: Curious," someone
who would unwind the twine, strip the paper—the peeling
      away of which would feel like tugs of rind from fruit,
thumbing that leaves the skin citrused. But, you see,
      you're not the locket in the middle of this nor the tape
keeping it together. Not the girl who mailed it all.
      Rather the flitting and fitting—a touch of tongue,
bee to bloom near season. The humming.

Daphne in the Rain

I'm walking through the streets of Rome, map in hand,
when it begins to rain—and not rain like you'd see

in *Roman Holiday* or *La Dolce Vita* where dresses
cling to women's bodies as if the sky chose

to dampen only their very best features, but
in pelting sheets that leave me looking like Romulus

or Remus' sheep dog half-drowned in the Tiber.
At every corner, vendors hold umbrellas and call

to me, but with only one more day abroad, I'll be damned
if I'm going to buy un *ombrello* just to leave it, so I repeat

Grazie, no, as I search for an alley to crouch in
while I try to piece together what's left of the map,

and a man approaches and begins gesturing, brandishing
an umbrella at me and muttering something in Italian

about the rain. I turn on him yelling, *Listen, jerk,
I don't need your damn umbrella! Leave me the hell alone,*

ready to whack him with my purse at another advance,
when stepping away he says, *Scusi. Mi dispiace. Umbrella*

for free. Pretty lady no get wet, his offering now dangled
in front of him in case I take his arm off with it. Releasing

my grip, I fumble to find some change, a few euros
but when I do, he's gone. Later in the gallery,

when I come upon *Apollo and Daphne*, I look for the motion,
the way the marble whirls into a fluttering mass of leaves

instead of stone, but what I see is a woman fleeing,
hurried into the transformation before his eyes.

The Hibiscus

—after Roethke

I can't uncurl crocus-like—my jaw doesn't slacken
     at the smell of bees or the clip
of oars through the Saginaw's pre-dawn stretch.
      Instead the constant noontime has made me
loose, a running-stitch meant to hold the hem
     for later thimble-taut handiwork.

I don't keep well—can't move from hothouse pot
      to window-box because I've never
learned the thrift of hard winters—frugal tuck of leaf
      and sun leaning. The Geranium survived
on alleyway scraps and shrieks, turned ashes
     to compost in an alchemy of muck.

She still got canned. Let the litany of my petals
      line your bin—I'd rather be that lonely.

The Mean Reds with Movie Lines

"When I'm good, I'm very good, but when I'm bad, I'm better."
—Mae West as Tira in *I'm No Angel*

No one notices but I'm plotting, and the tips
     of my fingers are keen for their part in the plan:
you see, *pal, I'm a busy little bee, full of stings*
     and that college co-ed—Kristi, Kathi, Tiffani,
(all those damn i's)—is going to get stung.
     I'll push her into a cactus bed and swipe her

caramel latte, cardboard coozie and all, because I'm
     that mean and it's a knock or be-knocked world
with limited choices: the door or the bronze knocker,
     both ringing with the phrase, *knock on any door*. But,
I won't Shirley Temple curtsy anymore—at some point
     we're too old for dancing in gauzy bloomers

and *animal crackers in our soup, loop-da-loop,*
     so *hit the road, buster—this is where you get off,*
because I've got overpasses to tag with pictures
     of elbows, ears, and feet dismembered DaDa-style,
and your rules are cramping my mojo, reigning
     in the glory of my *undies in the icebox*, merry-go-rounds

and cartwheels downhill. I'd ask you to join me,
     put your lips together and blow, rise up with a week's worth
of dirty laundry, pans crusted with leftover
     pasta pomodoro or adobo, but you won't do it
because you're kennel friendly, *your ship
     is in ship-shape shape*, you never lick the bowl.

But, *I'm ready for my close-up*: a Hollywood broad—
     a cigarette in one hand, booze in the other,
and a bob the kind a good Christian mother abhors—
     blowing smoke over my shoulder, saying, *Sugars,
I'm going on a tear*, and lickety-splitting it down
     Sunset or Mulholland, so *fasten your seatbelts,*

this is going to be a take all prisoners, hands out
          the vehicle, flip the bird joyride, and unless
the wheels come off, I'm gallivanting my way
          across the border, any border because *nobody puts*
baby in a corner, and my big dance number is next.
          So watch as this pin-up girl unpins herself,

flies the coop with her gal pal Winged Victory
          who's been pedestal stuck too long, because *men go*
to bed with Gilda and wake up with us, not Rita,
          just hussies and harlots from hometowns in Iowa,
Idaho, Ohio, holes in the lace of our panties,
          chipped finger nails in *jungle red* or *slutty secretary*—

until one morning soon, I'll stop Bill or Sam
          or James *(Call me Jim)*, and instead of the usual
number giving, fumbling, *See you next time. I had*
          a good time, I'll force his open mouth to mine,
kiss him full, and as I release, I'll bite his bottom lip—
          drawing blood so he knows the meanness of his own flesh.

Two

Relationship Status

> *Like as a huntsman after weary chase*
> *Seeing the game from him escaped away.*
> —Edmund Spenser

A date once texted me, hey u who u live with—no caps,
no period, no question mark—his attempt to start
a conversation, ask about the sock on the doorknob—
a more polite version of Craigslist's *DTF*
to which most people don't admit because that's taking
the silverware off the table, palm-scooping mashed potatoes
to mouth without a bib for the drippings. This shorthand,
the straight to go, do-not-collect 200-dollars, cuts out

the balcony crooning, skips the *Had we but world enough,*
and time, passes over me as hind or hart or deer—the prey
hunted and petted for flesh, underbelly soft and full.
Though I don't want to be stalked or arrow shot,
the bite of a flea might do the trick and lead to Donne-like
coaxing: *Thou know'st that this cannot be said a sin, or shame,*
and Johnny boy knew his girl was a Guinevere praying

to be jousted over, toasted with mead and nectar,
eaten like ambrosia because the gods, too, know
the down feather of a woman's touch and if Sirs Sidney
and Wyatt weren't careful, the big guys, the Henrys
4, 5 and 8 of the world, would've put her *fair neck round about:*
Noli me tangere. But, look, I don't take kindly to territory marking,
the mounting of fence posts and barbed wire, and there will be
no rings, no razors and toothbrushes left in my bathroom

during month one, but if a man leans on my doorbell
just right, wipes his feet clean on the mat, I'll come
to the peephole and peer out, look for the *thee's* and *thou's*
of his delivery pad because if he's got the package I've ordered,
he'll take a line from Bob Hicok's book and say, *Whither*
thou goest…[I] promise to be there conspicuously mad
in my devotion. Wild Bob kept the *whither,* the hand-made

valentine of magazine reds and toilet paper lace, a sign-arrow
that until nailed up means *You point the way*, and if I find
a man who'll hammer that sign to a post after he's blazed me
a trail in backpacking gear, drummed up a campfire,
and pitched a double-wide tent, I might *return the self-same way*,
collect lupine and Queen Anne's lace for my hair, melt
marshmallows over the fire, and waiting to hear his boots
on the wood-glen floor, let myself become his lynx, treed.

Dear Dr. Frankenstein

Invent me, would you, doctor dearest? Pull some secret
science out of your bag, read up on anatomy and frozen

fingers because I'll grease your palm, feel you up, even let you
paint my toes your favorite color and choose the dress I wear,

just not the itchy Bo Beep crinoline or the bonnet that covers
my hair because I've always wanted to show off a head of red,

like embers that need fanning or a Spanish terra cotta tiled roof.
When you're farming for parts, take Liz Taylor's lavender eyes

from her sockets and frame them with long eyelashes because
I'm not afraid of being fake, though I'd rather my boobs were real,

maybe from Lana Turner or Marilyn Monroe, and wrangle me a pair
of Rockette legs leading to Ginger Rodgers' feet because they'll help

me do what Fred did but backwards. Solder Hepburn's collarbone
on Isadora Duncan's torso, and make sure Queen Vicki's pinky

gets here from England so I can really drink a cup of tea.
C'mon and stick me together, I'll do the rest: catch fire

from a cigar, raise myself from your table, gut cities of men
who'll rush across suspended bridges, drag themselves over

open trenches for a chance with me, but I'll come back to you,
darling, just cut off an ear and sew it to me, bury a sixpence

in the sole of my foot, or if you really want me, make my navel
of lips so that at my center I can recognize your taste.

This Poem is For You

If I were a doctor, I'd put paddles to your chest,
     send blood bubbling and throbbing, feed it
with iron and IV, or I'd become a manicurist
    who carves the nails out of your flesh, singes
     the half moon shadows in their beds. I'd tend
your torso to shoulder ratio, weave the reeds
    of your ribs, snap the caps of your knees into place
     just to admire their shape, but since I can't, I'll be
your washerwoman and find you in the skin flecks
    and salt crust coating my basin, the bird enthusiast
     nosing around your yard trying to capture a look
of you through her binoculars, the candy cane
    maker who bends sugar to your liking. You see,
     before I met you, I was on another continent
and ate breakfast not knowing you existed. Today,
    you sleep so heavy and full I want to shake you,
     break off your eyelashes and knit them into
a prayer shawl I'll don when begging God to let you
    suck marrow from the air, teethe only on His knuckles
     and the handles of golden ladles. I want to crush you
to my chest, smother your breath to make you flail
    and kick because then I could save you, dot the i's
     of your being with a flourish of my pen, make-believe
I had a part in your creation, that you were mine.

On the Marquee

I never watch the end of *Gone with the Wind*
        because once Atlanta burns in a flurry of char
and hot iron and Rhett kisses Scarlett
    with the skyline mottled orange behind them,

I don't need to see any more—definitely
        not Nazis hunting the von Trapp family

out of Austria again. I've been in those hills,
    belted out, "Raindrops on roses, whiskers on kittens"
        on a sing-a-long tour through Salzburg
where I learned Christopher Plummer refused

    to carry Gretel, "that fat cow of a child,"
up the mountain for another take. And, when the bus
        dropped me off in a city park without a map
    or any idea which direction led to the hostel,

I felt six, the time my brother stomped
    on my Disneyland balloon, the mouse ears caving

into its mylar skull as I held onto the string,
        realizing that sometimes there is only one take,
    one set to burn down, and if we let go the string,
just before the kiss, we might be left

in a foreign city, the sound of water missing
        from wintering fountains, sculptures cloaked

in tarps, unrecognizable except for the postcards
    and snapshots for sale at the stands surrounding
the square. No, we don't need to watch the endings
        because we remedy that silence, fill it in,

the same way we imagine Norman's mother
    lurking in that basement before the chair swivels,

or the gasp we let go when, seconds ahead,
we realize that blind Audrey Hepburn, robbing

the screen of light, won't account for
                    the refrigerator bulb—its artificial glow

draping us as we grip the rough velvet
            of old theater seats, waiting in those seconds
                        before the scream. But then, somehow, it's our own
voices we hear, that sound sent up to delay

some future peril, postpone forays with henchmen thugs
            and escapes over Alps or Appalachians

because if we hang on past the second act,
                    we might discover that off screen
Clark Gable lost Carole Lombard, his love, in a plane crash
            and wish he could have stayed in Tara,
walked out on shrill Miss O'Hara over and over—

the popcorn trodden into the carpet as we exit,
            never again finding that name amongst the credits.

Far From Bushwick, The Next Mae West Announces Herself

"She's the kind of girl who climbed the ladder of success wrong by wrong."

I grew out of tarpaper and chicken wire, stuck sticks
                    to mud and called it adobe while you felt up bronze busts,
spit Brussels sprouts into peacock-shaped spittoons.

But before your past plumps you up, gets those
                    glass noodles boiling, I need to make one thing clear:
                                        you aren't slumming with me

because we both know I'm a prodigy, a real humdinger,
                    a hundred-dollar hotdog on a stick. And, though
your pedigree ducks and dodges the ink-fingered forgers

whose quills penned shifty titles and tender,
                    these, my ancestors, also grew penicillin, flew the Flyer
at Kitty Hawk, and, lover, that's just what you're in for:

needle pricks and cliffs because if you're in
                    for a dime, you're in for hocking your candelabras
and copper-bottomed pots from the backs

of bruised Pontiacs in asphalt-cracked lots. We need
                    this fire sale to free up hard drive space, distribute
our weight in puddle-jumper fashion, so that we two

might double-dutch through the tangles and brambles
                    of hungover mornings, toothpaste-less kisses. You won't
make it alone among broken bottle barbed wire,

won't see the beauty in *Fuckingassclownprepschoolsonsofbitches*
                    flung at auctioneer speed but cup my chin in your hand,
tilt my jaw until you find dirt speckling my irises:

their waters are no less blue. Dearest, our love
                    is a rope ladder hung over a snake-hissed pit—
                                        we've got some climbing to do.

Plate Appearances

Moose Stubing is the only major league player and manager never to register a hit or a win.

When Moose Stubing pinch-hit at the Big A in '67,
I bet he thought he'd finally made it into the can-do

category, left the bus leagues, the dive bars, the worn-out
Blue Star motels and Bob's Bungalows on the interstate
between Albuquerque and El Paso for bellhops and long-legged

women who come a-knocking at the door, but the gods
of designated hitters and pony leagues had other plans

and allowed him only five at-bats, four of them strike-outs,
marking zeros across his line. My father always questioned
that last trip to the plate, the one that wasn't a K, wanted

to picture a drive to left, fly ball to the warning track,
snowcone catch by the centerfielder stretched full length,

cap askew because then he could believe Moose made the most
of his shot, that there was a moment between dropping
the bat and running to first when he thought it had the distance,

because if he couldn't have the dinger or a double,
at least he was close, watching the ball cling to the drench

of late summer air in stadium lights, and it is the light
I remember, the way the newspaper caught the first ticks
of morning as I checked the columns, the records

of last night's outs, ribbies, and runs that my father cataloged
and we chewed on before he left for work. When he

recognized Moose at a game many years later, after I'd moved
from home, after my father was laid off the second time,
he almost didn't go over, didn't know if he could stand to have

that long fly ball turned into a squib or a can of corn but he did,
and Moose nodded, then said, "First pitch, ground out to short,

but I hit it *hard*," drawing out the last word like the threatening
of coyotes in the back hills, and that one word made it better
than the at-bat my father had long created and hung his hat on

because a grounder has grit, gets under your fingernails, sticks there
for a while like the sting of a first love lost or losing the last game

of the season in extra innings. When my father shook his hand
and said, "Glad to hear it, Mr. Stubing," he meant, "'Atta baby,"
"Leg it out, meat" because that swing was my father's almost,

his could've been, and Moose was his pinch hitter—traces
of dirt and pine tar, even now, staining both men's hands.

After My Cousin's Wedding

—Monteriggioni, Italy

Our friend Kristin doesn't think about drowning when she strips
        to her skin, jumps into the fancy Tuscan hotel's fountain

and begins posing like Venus on the half shell, the goddess's hair
        replaced by a shawl she flings as she reenacts the sea birth.

If we were at the more popular Trevi, she would be born
        on a bed of underwater lights and international coinage,

which makes me wonder who pulls out the change, all the thousands
        of euros, cents, dinars tossed into its basin for a chance

to come back, find love, marry an Italian. I like to think
        it's nuns or artists who wade into the water, scooping up

the money in pails or pie tins—they can use the alms
        we send over our shoulders, those holy and artistic types,

to save the world's souls or at least cover our sin in paint
        and incense. Once, my little brother fell in the fountain

at Mission Santa Barbara, came out dripping with a crown
        of algae, and I thought the water was sacred, the massive koi

really dewinged angels keeping watch over the building
        and its flock where Satan would never think to look.

I wanted to fall in, too, submerge myself and find salvation,
        or at least something like it, in the murky water. I'd still like

to get tipsy off its musk, attempt the great feat of my youth,
        be born again and again into a better life—that must be

what the Spaniards thought they discovered in Florida
        amid manatee and alligator. But if Ponce and his crew

came back now, a little drunk on adventure or ambition,
                they'd find neon arrows pointing the way to a ceramic fountain

whose electric blue depth promises unending futures,
                the souvenir t-shirts free with the price of admission,

while in Italy, they're hocking aprons of David full frontal,
                no grape leaf for modesty, and paper dolls you can dress

and undress in outfits from Botticelli classics,
                so maybe those keepsakes are the keys to this vita—

clothes laced with the potential for nudity
                or the soused revelry of an unprompted striptease—

only, as the newlyweds slip away hand in hand,
                I think it isn't that at all but something dangling

between *terra e cielo*, the language we'll never fully learn,
                the voices of lovers we may not have now
                                but could.

Date Five with the Luthier

An old guitar remembers every note it has played,
its wood vibrating open a little, the notes zinnia
petals in the city garden loosening with the clicks
of schoolboys' sticks against wrought iron fences.
If wood keeps those melodies, files them in a rolodex
of pitch and tension, then, lover man, make of the strings
a six-pleated tongue used to lick the air, tell your stories:
once, in the cab of your truck a girl, halter-topped,
dug a tick from your side, sucked on that rib-wound.
You must've liked it, her pluck and pull, half-steps,
the sharpness of novices, her mistakes written into you
like pounded iron. If ever my strumming stutters or slurs,
ease my fingers from chord to chord, gather yourself
around me: get a feel for the wood of me. Make me.

Ode to Kevin Costner in *Bull Durham*

Some men just know how to woo a woman,
      and you do, or at least you play men who do,
which is close enough for me because when you
      walk into that clubhouse, all leather jacket
and jeans, it's all I can do not to undress you,

      undo your buttons and mine, but I'll wait
because I've seen this one before and know
      that we'll end up in a bathtub dousing candles
with our overflow, you and me, that is, the Annie
      Savoy me, the better me who reads Whitman

to my lovers while they're bedpost lashed,
      who shows up to baseball games nyloned
and lipsticked, who collects men from the fray
      to craft them into show-worthy hitters as if my hips
controlled the thrust of bat, the slide into third.

      And this better me, this woman I'd like to be,
she extends her leg for you to unhook her garters
      with only one hand, and you do while applying
just the right amount of pressure to thigh
      and mean of back, making her, me, gasp-clutch

and so I replay it every year about this time
      when pitchers and catchers report to camp
and I think you would've liked to have been
      among them, the real you, the guy who played
ball in the fields near my house, who returns

      to see old coaches, throw out first pitches,
the man who, when he catches in the movie,
      reminds me of the boys I grew up with who dug
through ice-plant and chaparral for foul balls,
      the pony league players who fumbled with my bra

and zippers until I undid them myself. Yes, I think
                        you would've liked to have been a big-leaguer,
even a bus-leaguer, and tried your hand
            at some real stickball, taken up with a trollop
who'd wait for you to hit it big and take her

            with you. But the difference between us,
your would-be groupie and the me of the movie,
            is that I want to remind you of your sinew,
stake a place in your repertoire like the fingering
            of a two-seam fastball deep in the count.

But let's face it: Susan Sarandon, the actress,
            ended up with Tim Robbins, and all my Crash
Davises are pilots or brokers who take me
            to dinner on the company check, never knocking
dishes and milk from the counter as they make

            space to knead me against its tile as you would,
and if you knew me, the real me, you'd want me
            to let you because I'm that type of girl, the Annie
Savoy type who knows a full count from a hitter's
            pitch and can help you find the sweet spot

when you're slumping, because sometimes
            all we need is one summer to pant and sweat
and hammer it all out like we were the people
            we wanted to be when sex was on the screen
and we closed our eyes but felt it all anyway.

The Drive to Aeroporto Firenze

I can still see him standing in the window,
shirt open, untucked, too dark to make out
the countryside beyond his yard. I wondered
if a woman lay behind him, curled in bed,
negligee bunched around her breasts,
and I wanted to be her, to watch him pull on
his pants, tie his shoes, to pause with him
in the revelation of headlights before
kissing open mouthed in breaking day.

We've played the same scene, you and I,
except I'm eating Cheerios in your t-shirt
and you're looking over palm trees, sure
it's going to rain. I don't love you anymore
and you don't know that—where does love go?
Swept with dirt from the kitchen,
it must hang in the air outside our door,
waiting to be trod in again or washed away
for good. I wonder, will you forgive me this
because, like a storm, you knew this day
would come? Or will you punch the air in protest?

When I tell you, it will help me to think
of that Italian, his chest still damp from a shower
as he walks towards an open window to survey
his land, check on the grapes he tends, but then,
just then, he's drawn back to her, the woman
whose hair, rebellious on the pillow, summons
him to her side—their clutch the twine we let
slip into the half sighs and spilt wine of sundown.

Moving Targets

We're packing again, sending my boxes to the desert's
　　　　　　　sulking gila monsters, while yours are U-Haul-bound

for Oakland where citizens are rioting because a policeman
　　　　　　　shot a weapon-less black man—I read about a bystander

at that BART station tending to the fallen, how he knelt
　　　　　　　and listened to the heart still pumping but the blood tonguing

air instead of arteries, and when you tell me this happened
　　　　　　　down your future street, around the corner from where

the boxes we're filling in the garage-door light of evening
　　　　　　　will find their way, I think, we're conspirators

in death's master-plot—the ones using death's Sharpie to mark
　　　　　　　ourselves FRAGILE, BREAKABLE. But even if we are

the hit-men death keeps on contract, I'm still running from him
　　　　　　　because it's tough to hit a moving target and wrapping myself

in bubble wrap might cushion his blows. If I were brave,
　　　　　　　I'd stop, drill in molly-bolts, dare death to wring my neck

in the open of an Italian piazza because consent must last
　　　　　　　forever, and *yes, yes, yes* followed by *no* is still *no*. No, don't go.

Stay in my sight, and if you can't, if you must, I'll lick
　　　　　　　death's cheek, refill his cup, take him to my bosom and murmur

my pleas just long enough to give you a head start,
　　　　　　　because if we can't out-run him, at least we'll die trying.

Hard Times in the Tunnel-o-Love

I never planned to roll down the river of love alone,
      only a purse of Kleenex and hard candy mints

for company, but on this voyage the swan gondola ferries me,
      sans date, through a tunnel covered in love scenes

and just when Jack and Jill fall down the hill into each other's
      out-stretched arms and the life-size busts

of Bill, Hillary, and Monica start to glow, I notice the couple
      ahead of me rocking the boat so hard

it takes on water. They don't see the wall hung lovers—
      most post coital with trousers and dresses,

bras hanging on the limbs of cherub figurines that flit fake wings
      through the scenes. Along the way, King Henry

kisses the heads, and only the heads, of Anne and Kate,
      while Aeneas' sword repeatedly stabs

Dido on a pyre that combusts as each boat passes;
      the couples Cleaver & Petrie appear

in Andy Warhol brights on the two twin beds they've pushed
      together, now lying on stiff sheets

with chocolate chip cookie odor piped in, and exiting
      the tunnel, the water steeped

in artificial blue dye number 102, I look up to find Cupid
      staring down at me, his beady little eyes full

of judgment, which is when I envision myself: nearly-severed head,
      hole through the torso as if cannon-shot,

in bed, alone—and suddenly I want to paint my body on that wall
in love-bug blood, smear it across scant negligees

and puckered lips, dare the mannequins to keep undressing, caressing,
fucking each other—stop thinking of you.

Love Letters

—for Justin and Margaret on the occasion of their wedding

"Well, I suppose I have been writing something very foolish (to the world
at all events); but to us who love each other so dearly, it is not foolish at all."
–Wolfgang Amadeus Mozart to Constanze Mozart, 1789

If she were writing this, she'd begin,
When I sleep all covered with colors,
in a bed of pictures, and think
of the next tugboat hovering
in the space between buildings,
its rocking in that distance—bayed
but never still. And she'd imagine
the floor boards waiting for him, too,
and she'd tell them, *Nothing*
compares to his ears, his ears cold
like shells are cold, and the boards,
they'd reply, No, my dear, the ankles,
his knees. Yes, you're right, she'd say,
his joints that *I love to clasp with* mine,
that connect *all the paths of my nerves*
which are his because a year ago
he said, *How many things does 'to be with her'*
mean by now? The answer: she goblet
and he wine. Or perhaps, they two:
the bread and knife and tongue,
or none of it at all but the space
between lips. She wrote him once,
I think of you in Paris, in Paris
I miss you but he'd travelled with her
having collected his pieces
and sewn them into the binding
of *that book she always carried.*
And she, never wanting to be outdone
by his clever love, trimmed herself
out of seaweed and kelp,
washed to his shore and clung there,
bringing him the whale song

she'd learned in the deep—
at night, their warblings
tie knots, dear and foolish,
in the stretching salt air.

Calamity Jane Informs Wild Bill of His Faults While Visiting His Grave

I used to think there was no better smell than gun powder
              searing flesh, but turns out leather smeared with dirt
and sweat beats it, and you and me, we smelled a lot of it
         on each other briaring our way through the territory. I'm sure
you would've liked to see me strip out of a corset and bloomers,
              let the ribbon in my hair dust our foreplay, but I'm a two gun
woman and there's no place for a holster over calicos or ginghams—
         but dammit, Bill, if I can't still feel the calluses of your hands
hitching their way under my belt, your mustache blackberrying
              my neck and no one here believes me. They don't think I can
be all teacups and hatpins, and maybe I can't, but there's a place

         for spitting and cursing and carrying on, and it isn't
when you're Colt-pistol-crazy for a man. If you could,
              you'd tell them those letters to that woman in Ohio
were penned while knee deep in my saddle bags, tell them
         you loved the hoof-beaten trails of my torso, stream-stroked
trench of back—licking dirt, tinny and coarse, from between
              my breasts, but you ain't here to do the telling. I don't care
what people say, not my concern if their minds don't think
         about the world in colors, but I can't stop seeing it in the reds
that spilled with your brains on that poker table or the orange
         of vomit McCall retched when I went after him with a cleaver.

They won't see the purple of the dress I'll wear dead,
         but they'll dig me a grave next to yours and they'll have to swear
and spit to it, and then they'll believe me, they'll have to believe
              you loved me loosey tooth and tumbley all the way to the day
you got shot. I'd shoot myself now just to get near you again,
         mingle my rot with yours as we sour, but then they'd think
the only way I could land you was you forked and me begging
              and there's no truth to that, so I'll stay here near your marker,
wait them out watching the row of pines, the way they sway
         as if playing the last hand with a stacked deck, knowing it's all
going to fall my way so I'll take a long swig of whiskey and nod.

Three

The Tongue

I knew a girl at 10 who spent recess swinging open mouthed mixing
the wind with her hollers until one day on the dismount she misjudged
the height and slant of seat and when she hit the sand she bit her tongue
straight through and I think of that missing piece of tongue the taste of
flesh gone and her looking at it in the dirt as if it were a delicacy of cow
on a Hungarian menu a sack lunch she hadn't packed and later when
they stitched it back in her mouth the tongue turned purple filling the
space between her teeth as if demanding:

> *See if you can get rid of me again see*
> *if I won't bloat expand so that gums palette throat*
> *all feel my heft. See if you're glad someone picked me up*
> *washed off the blood and dirt and sewed me back*
> *on.*

To His Next Lover

Lick the skin behind his ear and tell me
           about his taste—salt and soap, do we
agree?—and the smell of his breath
           in the morning, like yeast dissolving
in milk, and the way his mouth peels back
           like the pulled edge of a nosey neighbor's
curtain. You slept with him last night,
           and now, I keep picturing you
beneath him in the back of our high school
           auditorium among the painted backdrops
of the New York skyline where his spread hand
           palms your inner thigh and head back,
chest out, you can see the stars painted
           on canvas behind him. For weeks
I found stars in a cluster of white watermelon seeds,
           the unfilled spaces of crossword puzzles,
the holes in saltines; imagined them
           in the slants of light through eucalyptus
branches, chain-link fences; tried coaxing starlight
           to me with prayers to moon gods, but you
probably don't even believe in *fortuna*. I bet you see
           only plywood and paint, but you'll sleep
with him again, of course, this time in the back
           of his car on an LA street. Don't bother
looking up because you'll never find the stars
           through the smog, the city's glare, cars moving
their drivers towards garages, dinners,
           lovers whose names they'll never know.

Sarah Winchester's Sestina in Thirteens

The Winchester Mansion in San Jose, CA was under continuous construction for 38 years.

I said, *I don't want to die*, and my psychic
           said, *Then build. As long as you're building,*
you'll be living, so I sold the Boston house,
           went west, laid the foundation without a plan
because she promised it'd bring redemption
           to my family for the rifles, the angry dead
seeking revenge, retribution for their deaths
           and I try to tell them, at least psychically
that I regret our share of guilt, that redemption
           is all I seek, that when we started building
the business, vengeance was never the plan,
           so I've put the gun money into this house.
It's theirs, too, this ever-expanding house

locked in a California valley among dead
           oaks, fence posts put on hills without a plan,
where I'll ask for a hayloft because my psychic
           didn't specify how many rooms to build
or if repainting counted towards redemption,
           but I'm sure the new portico is redemptive,
unlike the more utilitarian add-ons: outhouses,
           sheds. The spirits don't molest the builders,
don't wrinkle their tarps, don't create dead-
           ends and booby traps. Sometimes, psychically,
I can sense them eavesdropping on the plans
           I try to hammer out, but I'm still planning
closets, cupboards stocked with redemption

for those rifle-shot souls caught in the psychic
           confines of curses and hexes. It's only a house
made of redwood shingle, glass, but the dead
           hunt me here, lurk and crouch in this building
as they do in my dreams where the night builds
           to a voice telling me to keep creating, planning
until thirteen red doors open onto thirteen dead

bodies in thirteen clawfoot bathtubs, redemption
drowning in the tepid water. I'm begging, House,
save me from my fate. If you'll only let the psychic
vibrations help me build, construct the houses
of my afterlife in blueprints psychically planned
for redemption, then I can stay one nail ahead of death.

How to Be Lonely

I'm mad   not angry but mad   mad
in the sense of Lady MacBeth or Kathy Bates
in *Misery*   which is to say equal parts loon
& fume   but for now I'm just plain   mad
and so I've written it   near the spine
at the center of books (not mine or yours but
ones left lying on diner counters)   I'm mad
scrawled it along the edges of unused subway
passes   I'm mad   scribbled it on dollar bills
drug store receipts   the backs of paintings
that when hocked or sold or rehung will
declare   I'm mad   And you should know
because you are   the one   I'm mad at
you're the ruiner   quarreler   screwer of all
my ambitions   to string spoons across the
Golden Gate   their round faces   reflecting
my madness   from perches above a bay full
of gold-miners' sunken shovels and shark
teeth   If only you'd be mad   full of fists
and flying fucks   or mad   so mad
you'd yowl long belly vowels into my mouth
bury my keys   in pig entrails   dismantle
my collarbone   that coat hanger of the chest
keeper of width & cavity   then   madder
than mad   you would fill stuff cram pack us
us two   into our get-away *Ape Cinquecento*
so we could put-put to plains that sun
themselves out past city limits but you don't
won't   give me that route path causeway
to gone long gone   and so late last night
just-coppered dogwood   out my window
I folded myself into fall's first heavy quilt
fingered the seams between paisley &
gingham until I forced   stripe and shape
my arteries   their beating   to hush blend
meld my thrumming   to the stillness of you

An Affair of Letters, with Pro Wrestling and Foreign Tongues

You see, dear heart—can I call you that? Too much and not enough
for a man I know only in letters—I didn't grow up on the road,

stalks of corn framed by a backseat window with only a father up front,
and I don't know those heroes of yours, the ones whose names rhyme

and ricochet when announced over speakers into the ring: Macho Man,
Stone Cold Steve Austin, Hulk Hogan, but I can see the appeal of their high flying

slams, the Main Event hijinks that cause their exposed veins to tense and bulge,
and I picture you, the boy-you, watching an old TV from a motel room floor—

your eyes bouncing from the men's primary colored costumes to their women
perched ringside in skintight, sequined dresses. I imagine the now-you admiring

the cut of your arms in the gym mirror the same way the wrestlers might,
the way I too eye photos of you for that, the hardness that comes from worked

muscle under skin, but more, the way your mouth is set—appraising,
resolved. The world is full of metal chairs flung to the back of the head

and straight-armed clotheslines that drop us to the floor, and you know this
much more than I do. Maybe that's what draws you to them, these thickened men—

despite the drama of throwing the opposition through a table, they all walk away
from the fight to beers and ice baths, their fame housed in sturdy, stocky bodies

and choreographed comebacks. But for me, stripped of the script that calls
for each *bam, pop, pow,* and *kabam,* their blows seem muffled, too quiet, the skin

on skin contact—rough and painful and real—missing. And that seems
partly our problem: the distance between our bodies, the fact you can't

frame my face with your palms, feel my curls soft against your hand
as we lay in bed and whisper. In the light, we've created our own loneliness,

lived like your wrestlers: too strong and alone, too strung out on the plotlines
we've invented for ourselves, enamored with versions of the world we don't know

are true or possible. For now, touch me. If you touch me the way your words do
with the force of all caps and exclamation, with gentle breaths on my neck

between sentences, if you stroke my skin with your lips just as foreign languages
seep into the backgrounds of your travel stories, *s'il vous plait* and *dankeschön,*

maybe we'll find there's enough between us for an era—short but full of glitz—
before our knees give out, before we lose each other in the commotion that follows

when someone else wins the belt—someday our pull will be only a fondness
of the past, the video aired every ten years in commemoration of the hubbub

and hiccup our figures, sweaty and prime, made by chucking ourselves into the fray
—aiming for arms stronger than our own that might hold us through the night.

To Grace, A Friend's Daughter

—East Tennessee Children's Hospital, Knoxville, TN

You gasped life in the falling
                  light of Tallahassee oaks—
your mother using the cutlery
                  of our late lunch to play doctor:
first, fork as the needle seeking
                  ovaries, then knife, the catheter
that appended you into her.
                  And though we've never met,
you held me there, round the neck,
                  to whisper of the harvesting
from which you were stitched.
                  I knew I couldn't then clasp
the water-filled cups of your tea parties,
                  couldn't carve a rocking horse arc
out of reclaimed elm, couldn't locate
                  the rope your parents scaled
to discover you in the nests
                  of their bodies. Instead, I held
the napkin of your make-believe womb,
                  dabbed it to my lips, and tried
to smell you in the ether
                  of your mother's telling.

               ***

Since the storms, I've begun
                  to sleep in the bathtub—
its smallness curls me in
                  where the wind at the windows
cannot cut me. I cling to quilt
                  and slumber, thinking this is where
I'd like to keep you
                  with your bald-again head
because it's the closest thing I know
                  to the cigar box in which I tucked

the baby doll my grandmother made me
                        out of muslin and old socks. As a child,
I'd close the lid, slide the box
                        under the corner of my bed, and listen
for the secrets I believed
                        the baby uttered, snug in the buttons
and hair-bows of her sleep.

                              ***

Scientists can now suck out
                        the DNA of regular house cats
and replace it with the code
                        for the rarer Arabian sand breed,
and I wonder, do the mothers know
                        their kittens are only partially
their own, separated from them
                        by letters in the genetic alphabet?
Or do they, in suckling the young,
                        find only the tug of nipple,
feel only their own milk
                        pulled from them?

                              ***

I want you to have the tousling
                        of Florida tangerine trees,
chiffon swirls in full-skirted
                        dresses, Blues beats
hung on your headboard,
                        traced over the hills rising behind
your Tennessee yard. For you,
                        the hot air balloons that dot the dusk
of my horizons, the glow-bug evenings
                        on your grandparents' porch,
the slow sip of sail into harbor.
                        So, hold tight, little one, as you scramble

out onto that log. We're too ground-tied
                    to climb across with you, too heavy
to tread out that far, but hanging back
                    we'll strain to see your feet finding
holds in the knots and pockmarks
                    of trees downed across gullies,
your steps ginger then steady and true.

The Sunlight of Our Own House in the Forest

–after a line from Randall Jarrell, "A Man Meets a Woman in the Street"

I want to stand in the wings of your life unlit while you take center stage,
recite a poem, tell a joke, leap Pavlova-like into the foot lamps
as the house gasps in delight, the audience clinging, desperate to hold you,
to mold your presence into a porcelain doll easily carried in the palms

of their star-crazed hands. I want them to watch your mouth, lips that dip
to mine mid-sentence, the way my hand moves hip to waist untying
your apron, halts the pulse of your vibrato rising to Billie Holiday's
"God Save the Child" in our sauce-stained kitchen—your voice off key,

mouth laced with tomato. I want your outline to stop translating
to pentameter, your lilt to drown out the rhymed couplets I'm revising
in the spaces between our tête-à-tête. Just for a moment, I want to stand
next to you in line at the market and hear your shallow breath instead

of caesura. I want to hold hands with your shadow, unnoticed, to skip
in your wake as you walk up Main Street towards McClintock's
old tavern on those Saturday nights. I want everyone to turn as you
stride by, point out your Katharine Hepburn tilt and gait. But more, I want

the foreman on our farm to rush home to his wife after a late night,
get cursed by an apple-truck driver he nearly hits in his hurry. She'll know
something happened, but won't ask, waiting for him to tell her you died,
and they'll mourn. I want to die first, you stepping unfettered into that light.

Under the Condor

—Santa Barbara Natural History Museum, CA

1.
The feathers, dust-covered and thinning,
are not the wet ebony they once were,
and my grandmother knows this.

2.
The ranger brings the hail-struck carcass
to the schoolyard over the mountain—
spreads her on her back at full mast,
shows her off—the massive wingspan,
the talons bigger than workmen's boots.

My grandmother wriggles through the crowd
until she stands only a foot away, staring
into one bloodshot eye. In it, she sees
a pale-aqua egg perched in a cliff's crevice,
feels a draft, warm and lulling—her arms
tug at her as if wings meant for flight.

3.
The condor, wrapped in a tarp, is deposited
in the back of a pick-up. Later, she's razed
and stuffed, stuck with wires, and hung
in the gallery below a cloud painted sky.

4.
For weeks, she swallows the growls and hisses
she means to hurl at the other little schoolgirls—
doesn't ask them to beak-push rocks, play tug
of war with carrion, taste dirt and blood.

But she wants to, wants to answer the condor
she hears from within the eye, wants to find
that sound within her gut and reply in howls
passed through a teeth-clinched mouth.

5.
I found her in the bird room, amid nests
perched on a sawed-off fence post, woven
on a navel orange, dug into the hard dirt
of drought. My grandmother would take me
there—the smell of death carefully stowed
behind glass-fronted cabinets, tucked in
the taxidermist's stitches and stuffing.

6.
She still hangs, and I've come back to stand
under her patchy underbelly, the red of her bare
head shining in the bulb-light as it has for 50 years.

Before I stop myself, my lips part in a prayer
of grunts that her marble eyes seem
to understand—I ask for what my grandmother
would've wanted, what I now want: *Take me,*
hang me in the last of your blinking, and I almost
confuse our forgiveness for the thermostat's hiss.

What I'll Settle For

I'll settle for Belle Starr's black velvet cape
       cascading over the spotted rump of a mustang
as I ride sidesaddle away from a stagecoach heist
       with the usual money but also the trunks marked
for Bull's Head Saloon filled with red satin ruffles
       on dancing girl dresses, because I want to strut down
Main Street with big hair and heels, too-red lipstick
       and kiss you dead on the mouth without a greeting,
because if I were that woman, the one whose bureau
       is filled with wigs and whips and naughty French maid
costumes, you'd still want me in greedy handfuls
       that leave you sucking your fingers for the taste
of my shampoo and sunscreen, and then, suddenly
       overcome by my boldness, I could stop loving you
and spit out your residue like the splintered sunflower
       seed shells that whittle, razor, honey my tongue.

Kinky Love Poem

Good Morning America reports men find
straight hair more attractive, preferring
to stroke it, slide their fingers through
the rippleless layers as if hair corresponds
to the smoothness of a woman's curves,
the length of her legs, the pull of her
arched back, and I wonder if men
around the world feel similarly,
because a man I met in Italy took
a handful of my curls and said, *You could lose
an arm in this*, followed by, *It smells nice, though*,
and I laughed because I'd heard it before
in the perfect English of other men who later lay
in my bed to twist curls, letting them corkscrew off—
leading me to wrap 38 inches
of leg around their torsos, coiling us together.
After, elbow propped, these men reach out to press
my hair to pillow—attempting to still a field
of meteors, corral kudzu vines—only the curls
expand at their touch, unravel into a frizzled fan
not unlike a head of snakes, which is what
my classmates thought in middle school
when they called me Medusa, my hair matted into something
viscous and wild, as if the gorgon reincarnated herself
into curly-headed women everywhere,
dooming us to an existence ruled by
the inconsistencies of wind and humidity.
But, in token of her love for our winding tresses,
she also left us her power—somewhere tangled
in the thickness of my hair are pieces of rock,
remnants of old lovers turned to stone
by the very strength of my love.

NOTES

"The Hibiscus": This poem is a response to Theodore Roethke's "The Geranium."

"The Mean Reds with Movie Lines": Language in this poem is derived from movie lines indicated by italics. The films referenced appear in this order: *Breakfast at Tiffany's, All About Eve, Knock on Any Door, Curly Top, Nine to Five, The Seven Year Itch, To Have or Have Not, Some Like It Hot, Sunset Boulevard, All About Eve, Dirty Dancing, The Women,* and *Blazing Saddles.*

"Relationship Status": This poem incorporates lines from Edmund Spenser's "Amoretti LXVII: Like as a Hunstman," Andrew Marvell's "To His Coy Mistress," John Donne's "The Flea," Sir Thomas Wyatt's "Whoso List to Hunt, I Know where is a Hind," and Bob Hicok's "Whither Thou Goest."

"On the Marquee": The films *The Sound of Music, Psycho,* and *Wait Until Dark* are mentioned in this poem but not by name.

"Far From Bushwick, The Next Mae West Announces Herself": The quote used as an epigraph is attributed to Mae West.

"Love Letters": Lines from love letters and poems are incorporated into this poem and indicated by italics. In order of appearance, the writers include Marc Chagall, Katherine Mansfield, Frida Kahlo, Franz Kafka, Billy Collins, Simone De Beauvoir, and Billy Collins.

This collection would not exist without the support of a host of mentors and friends. Kevin Clark first opened the door to poetry and helped me believe I could walk through it. David Kirby taught me, with equal parts wisdom and humor, how to ensure that "the poetry store is always open." I'll always be indebted to Barbara Hamby who showed me how to live a life full of beauty, art and generosity. My writing group in Tallahassee (Laura Newton, Jen McClanaghan, Deborah Hall, and Christine Poreba) provided me with true poetic companionship that echoes even now. In Dominika Wrozynski I found a friend whose suggestions and advice continue to buoy my work. My workshop classmates at Florida State University, especially friends Avni Vyas & Eric Lee, helped these poems along in their earliest stages, and later, workshop classmates at Arizona State University helped polish and refine them. Cynthia Hogue models how to make one's own way with grace and force—I'll be forever grateful for her patience and kindness. The poetic kinship with Rachel Andoga and Sara Sams kept me writing and revising while in the desert, both literally and figuratively. Annie Dawson shared her talents in getting these poems out into the world. Profound thanks to all.

Never-ending gratitude to the two girls on the cover and the women they became: Betty Alcorn, my great aunt, and Barbara Ford, my grandmother. I hope I've inherited a small measure of your determination, grit, kindness, and humor. You inspire me. I was lucky to have fierce, smart women to watch growing up—these poems are due in large part to the Ford women, whether by blood or in spirit.

Affection and gratitude to my parents Scott and Leslie Grieve for loving me so completely that they let me pursue every opportunity. And, finally, deepest love to Adam whose belief in me and our life together spurs me ever on.

Sarah Grieve is an accidental sun follower—living in California, Florida, Arizona, and California again. She's been lost in every major city she has ever visited and finds that is the best way to see the world and write about it. As a child, she wanted to be a dentist, an orphan, and a princess—all at the same time. She loves Broadway musicals and classic Hollywood. Her lifetime free throw percentage is better than Wilt Chamberlain's, but that's not saying much. She has been known to cry at television commercials, book acknowledgments, greeting cards, and movie previews. Sarah's future will certainly include club sandwiches, Cleveland sports, and a German shepherd named after a president. Her great grandmother used to say, "Don't bother telling a story if you're not going to embellish it."

www.ingramcontent.com/pod-product-compliance
Lightning Source LLC
Chambersburg PA
CBHW021202090426
42740CB00008B/1204